Celebrating the City of Paris

Walter the Educator

Silent King Books

SILENT KING BOOKS

SKB

CELEBRATING THE CITY OF PARIS

Copyright © 2024 by Walter the Educator

All rights reserved. No part of this book may be reproduced in any manner whatsoever without written permission except in the case of brief quotations embodied in critical articles and reviews.

First Printing, 2024

Disclaimer
This book is a literary work; the story is not about specific persons, locations, situations, and/or circumstances unless mentioned in a historical context. Any resemblance to real persons, locations, situations, and/or circumstances is coincidental. This book is for entertainment and informational purposes only. The author and publisher offer this information without warranties expressed or implied. No matter the grounds, neither the author nor the publisher will be accountable for any losses, injuries, or other damages caused by the reader's use of this book. The use of this book acknowledges an understanding and acceptance of this disclaimer.

Celebrating the City of Paris is a souvenir book that belongs to the Celebrating Cities Book Series by Walter the Educator. Collect them all and more books at WaltertheEducator.com

PARIS

In the embrace of dawn's gentle whisper,

Paris

A city stirs, where dreams and echoes fuse,

Paris

Paris, the eternal muse, where lovers linger,

Paris

Streets adorned with tales, ancient and new.

Paris

Cobblestones, kissed by history's tread,

Paris

Underneath the sha

Paris

Whispering secrets of the long-gone dead,

Paris

In the rhythm of the Seine's soft breeze.

Paris

Montmartre's hills rise with fervent grace,

Paris

Artists' haven, where creativity flows,

Paris

Brushstrokes and verses find their sacred space,

Paris

In bohemian winds that eternally blow.

Paris

Charming cafés with laughter and sighs,

Paris

Espresso and croissant in morning's glow,

Paris

Conversations floating, beneath azure skies,

Paris

As Notre-Dame stands guard, steadfast below.

Paris

Eiffel's iron lattice, reaching to the stars,

Paris

A beacon of elegance, wrought in steel,

Paris

Illuminating nights, seen near and far,

Paris

A symbol of romance, palpable and real.

Paris

Champs-Élysées, a boulevard of dreams,

Paris

Where couture and class embrace and dance,

Paris

Windows glittering with opulent gleams,

Paris

Inviting hearts to dream and chance.

Paris

Hidden alleys, quiet as a lover's touch,

Paris

Reveal the soul of Paris in whispers slight,

Paris

Bookstores and bistros that mean so much,

Paris

To poets and dreamers lost in the night.

Paris

The Louvre's grand halls, a treasure trove,

Paris

Mona Lisa's smile, enigmatic and wise,

Paris

Echoes of ancient worlds in statues rove,

Paris

History framed in every passerby's eyes.

Paris

Along the Seine, barges float with ease,

Paris

Mirroring the skies, changing yet serene,

Paris

Reflections of bridges, arches that seize,

Paris

Moments of eternity in a fleeting scene.

Paris

So let us wander, through streets old and new,

Paris

With open hearts and eyes that seek,

Paris

In Paris, the city where dreams come true,

Paris

And love's eternal flame never grows weak.

Paris

ABOUT THE CREATOR

Walter the Educator is one of the pseudonyms for Walter Anderson. Formally educated in Chemistry, Business, and Education, he is an educator, an author, a diverse entrepreneur, and he is the son of a disabled war veteran. "Walter the Educator" shares his time between educating and creating. He holds interests and owns several creative projects that entertain, enlighten, enhance, and educate, hoping to inspire and motivate you.

Follow, find new works, and stay up to date
with Walter the Educator™
at WaltertheEducator.com

Milton Keynes UK
Ingram Content Group UK Ltd.
UKHW020742080724
445166UK00012B/184